CONTENTS

Introduction

This collection of poems was written during a period of twenty years. Each poem is written with depth, simplicity, and substance, or meat. I know some poems are short and quick reads, but there is meat, or substance, in each poem and each word. It is written to cradle and pierce the spirit, never leaving you the same but changed, and made whole and different.

Learning to Love Yourself

You never learned to love the body the Lord blessed you with.
Jesus gave you a healthy body, but you constantly devise ways to destroy it because you don't love yourself.
You smoke, drink, do drugs, mutilate it, allow others to use your body, and allow others to harm your body repeatedly.
You even attempt to kill your body by suicide.
You curse the day you were born.

Jesus will teach you to love the body you live in because Jesus loves you just as you are.
Jesus created you. Why would He hate His creation?
You can be blessed in the body you have.
You can love yourself just as Jesus does.
Then you will learn to love others despite their outer appearance.
The Word of the Lord reads, "Man looks at the outward appearance but the Lord looketh on the heart" (1 Samuel 16:7).

I love Jesus!
September 8, 1999

Soulmate

The issue is not whether a man can make me feel good or make me laugh.
The issue is, will he make a good Christian husband?

Will he be a faithful churchgoer?
God-fearing, on his knees praying, every pay-check tithe-paying, caring, and sharing husband?

Will he be the head of the household, in control, Bible-reading, Holy Ghost–filled, and an interceding husband?

Always understanding, never demanding, loving, and a thinking-of-me kind of husband?

Overcoming evil with good; providing for the home as he should; walking in the Spirit, not in the flesh, confident in himself to do the best?

This is a soulmate with a soul of life, spiritually grounded in Jesus Christ!
I love the Lord! Thank You, Jesus!

October 11, 1999
1:22 PM

Cruise of a Lifetime

I was on the cruise of a lifetime—a cruise filled with love, life, joy, and peace. The halls were filled with sanctification, and the rooms with anointing. And the deck was decorated with the gusting wind of a sweet spirit. Intercession was made three to four times daily. This cruise was an unusual journey of longevity, intimacy, and intensity. It seemed that He and I were out at sea for over seven hundred days. I hoped this cruise would never end. There were so many glorious times on this cruise, and best of all, the fare was free! This cruise was propelled by an everlasting force and was on an undefeatable course. I looked forward to being out to sea every day on this cruise until one night.

The cruise was abruptly sent off course because there was a sailor in an abandoned ship looking for shelter. This sailor seemed to be the best of the fleet, surely the cream of the crop! Having the sailor aboard created an imbalance on the cruise. The usual program decreased enormously. A cruise that once had navigation no longer had a navigator or a compass. This sailor, who so wonderfully presented himself, was now becoming comfortable aboard the ship. It seemed that a few months passed, and the sailor had completed his mission. It was time to leave and resume former tasks.

By now, the cruise was off course and eventually had to be docked. I was now off the ship. I lifted the hem of my garment to prevent it from being soaked by the water. It was useless! I was shipwrecked and left standing in still shallow waters. As I stood there in awe, I reminisced about the days on that magnificent cruise. As I stood in the waters, the *waves* began to splash upon my ankles, gradually approaching my knees and soon to reach my waist. The *waves* created turbulence every day, just SPLASHING and WHIPPING my back and legs. They were *waves* of the future, present, and past; *waves* of yesterday, today, and forever. As I stood in the still, shallow waters, looking into the abyss of my circumstances, I wondered when the Captain of the ship would come to rescue me again on the cruise of a lifetime.

July 18, 2000
9:35 PM

Through the Fire

I had to go through the fire to become who
I am today.
Experience the hurt, disgust, and pain.
Feel the flames and get drenched by rain.

I had to go through the fire to test my soul,
monitor my control, and weld broken
pieces back into a whole.

I had to go through the fire to realize what
was stole, to seek seraphims that could

bring live coals, hoping to be cindered
and refined into pure gold.

I went through the fire to test my limitations
through various trials and tribulations
just to learn that God's grace is not
imitation.

Praise the Lord!

January 17, 2001

Remember Winter

Remember winter, when the sun hid behind
the clouds.
Remember winter, when Jack Frost spoke out
loud.
Winter was a time when the pressure was
high and spirits were low.
Feelings were suppressed, and emotions were
covered with snow.
The icy cold words were like pins and needles
in my head.
I wished for warmth but received coldness
instead.

Although the winter is over, I still feel cold
because the winter is in me, captivating
my mind and hindering my soul.

April 30, 2001
10:23 PM–10:32 PM

Son Rise

Come to my aid.
Hear me cry.
Quench my soul…with the reasons why.
I have been in the dark, searching for the moon with an open, empty hand.
I reach up…hoping for your rescue soon.
Thank You for the refreshing.
Thank You for the renewing.
I have to thank You that I'm making it
In all that I am pursuing.
Like a dove, I am gentle.
Like a serpent, I am wise.

But give me the strength
And new armor to make it until the sunrise.
I ask and I pray…that the Son shall rise.
May the Son of God…rise! Rise! And deliver
me.

Friday, December 17, 2010
10:39 PM–10:52 PM

Walking on Scattered Pieces

When I make it to shore through these muddy waters, I will say I made it on broken pieces. But first, I must place one foot in front of the other on scattered pieces in the water. The yellow pieces represent happiness and joy. I try to stand on those as long as I can. However, there are other pieces, such as black ones, where I sometimes sit and rest in my sorrow. Then I get up and stretch my right foot toward the green pieces. The green pieces tell me I can go forward. "I can make it! It's going to be all right! Lift your head!"

But I turn and look back at the black pieces and place my left foot on a grey piece while I tell myself, “You are a soldier! You can make it!” Yet I’m apprehensive and alone, and my sword is lying on the ground. Then I reach the red pieces. These represent the blood of Jesus. These are the pieces that will take me to shore. This piece is strong, sturdy, and without doubt. I know I am saved and made whole by the blood of Jesus, to conquer my broken pieces and to mend my broken life. For He has made me whole!

Inspired by Acts 27:44
March 21, 2011
11:43 PM

I Come Forth

I have broadened my mind to the beauty that
is before me.
It's something so useless yet useful.
I come forth powerful with a rough edge but
soft enough to receive the gifts at hand.

I come forth pushing doors off hinges, standing erect, no sweat, confidence benefits with no fringes.

I come forth for the fourth time, knowing who I am, redeeming my time, working to refine, no need to define.

I come forth continuing to know right from wrong, still strong, knowing where I belong, not going to compromise, and not afraid to be alone.

I come forth standing in love, standing in peace, being filled with wisdom, and partaking of the feast.

I come forth from the inside out. I admire who I am, no titles involved. I love my spirit and give thanks to those who were negative, positive, and helped me evolve. I am worth more than my weight in gold. So tell the real estate agent, "This temple is sold!"

I come forth even on my worst day, loving the beautiful woman on the inside and the outside. I never give up on myself. I never hurt myself. I love and respect myself. My love is not based on lashes, eyebrows, clothes, nails, and hair. My love doesn't fluctuate based on my happiness or despair.

I come forth with substance, saying what I mean and meaning what I say.

I come forth with the bread of sincerity and truth, with strength, faith, abundance, integrity, honesty, high self-esteem, and security.

But most of all, I have a promise of blessed assurance because of Him in me.

August 18, 2011

Through A Glass, Darkly

For now we see through a glass, darkly.
But then face-to-face, we see our reflection through a glass, darkly.
We hope for clarity through a glass, darkly.
We sing songs with a black-tinted microphone.

Our innocence is lost at a ripe, tender age.
We live, love, and like through filters of
suspicion, distrust, malice, and rage.

Broken dreams and broken promises put a crack in my glass as I pacify myself with words such as "This too shall pass."

We rate ourselves; we hate ourselves, sedate ourselves, and make ourselves suffer the unnecessary reflection of ourselves through a glass, darkly.

May God keep His angels around to guard me.
I look for blessings as the Lord rewards me.
Not dwelling on the bling-bling! Or the sparkly!
But I'm still encouraged as I see through a glass, darkly.

Inspired by 1 Corinthians 13:12
Monday, September 19, 2011
11:00 PM

Synopsis

The strength, the tears, the minutes, the
years, the hope, and the fears.
Problems seem bigger than they appear.

Tuesday, October 29, 2019
8:30 AM

About the Author

Stephanie Davis was born in the Midwest. She is a degreed professional with master's level coursework in industrial organizational psychology and human resources management. Davis graduated with a bachelor of science degree in psychology, with a minor in criminal justice, from Missouri State University. She pursued a master's level education in industrial organizational psychology at Roosevelt University in Chicago, Illinois, and enrolled in human resources management classes at Webster University.

Davis began writing poetry in her early adulthood. As a Christian, she is creative and possesses a healthy, broad sense of humor. She has spent most of her career in human resources, writing poetry in her spare time as she found inspiration through God and the guidance of the Holy Spirit. Davis enjoys dancing, watching reality television shows, writing in her spare time, and taking beautiful, interesting photos of nature and flowers.

www.ingramcontent.com/pod-product-compliance
Lightning Source LLC
LaVergne TN
LVHW021130160826
845679LV00015B/1703

* 9 7 9 8 8 9 1 3 0 8 6 8 8 *